Teaching Little Fingers to Play More Christmas Carols

Piano Solos With Optional Teacher Accompaniments
By
Carolyn M

T0078914

CONTENTS

12603

It Came Upon the Midnight Clear
Optional Teacher Accompaniment

Arr. Carolyn Miller

Smoothly

with pedal

It Came Upon the Midnight Clear

Edmund H. Sears

Richard S. Willis
Arr. Carolyn Miller

Play both hands one octave higher when performing as a duet.

Smoothly

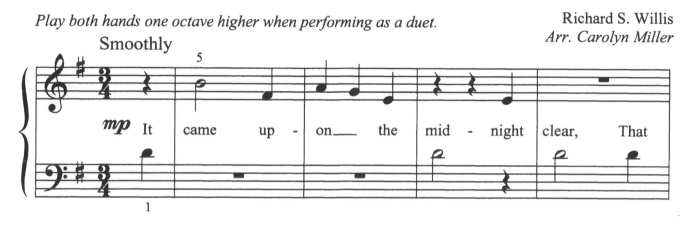

mp It came up - on___ the mid - night clear, That

glo - rious song___ of old,_____ From

an - gels bend - ing near the earth To

touch their harps___ of gold:_____ "Peace *mf*

12603

Optional Teacher Accompaniment

on the earth,— good - will to men From

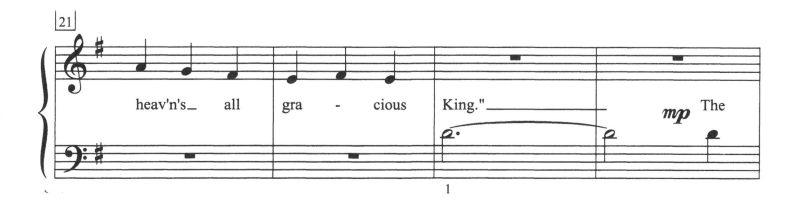

heav'n's— all gra - cious King."——————— *mp* The

world in sol - emn still - ness lay To

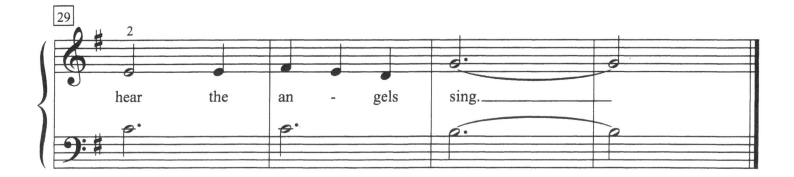

hear the an - gels sing.————

Go, Tell It on the Mountain
Optional Teacher Accompaniment

Arr. Carolyn Miller

Joyfully

Go, Tell It on the Mountain

Play both hands one octave higher when performing as a duet.

Swing

African-American Spiritual
Arr. Carolyn Miller

Joyfully

Optional Teacher Accompaniment

Joy to the World!
Optional Teacher Accompaniment

Arr. Carolyn Miller

Joyfully

Joy to the World!

Isaac Watts

Play both hands one octave higher when performing as a duet.

George F. Handel
Arr. Carolyn Miller

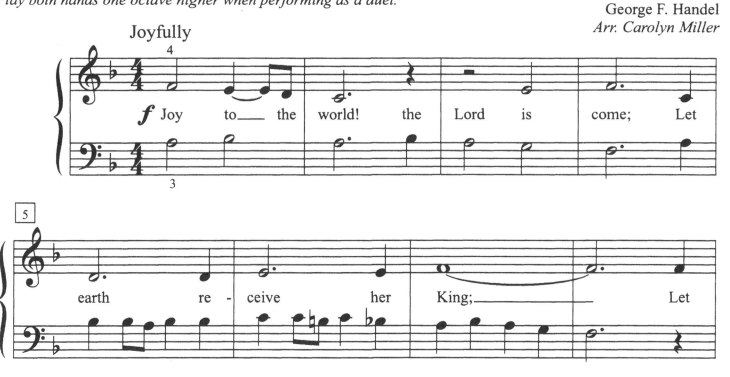

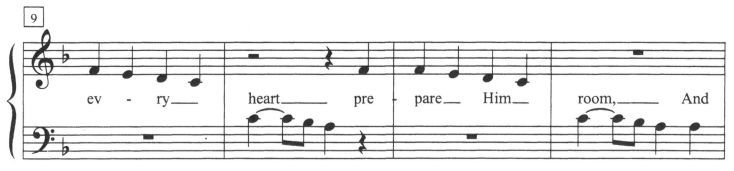

Away in a Manger
Optional Teacher Accompaniment

Arr. Carolyn Miller

Tenderly

p

with pedal

rit.

Away in a Manger

Martin Luther

Carl Mueller
Arr. Carolyn Miller

Play both hands one octave higher when performing as a duet.

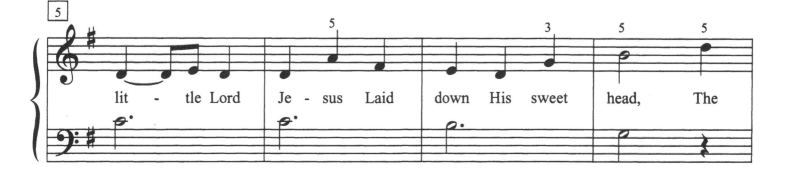

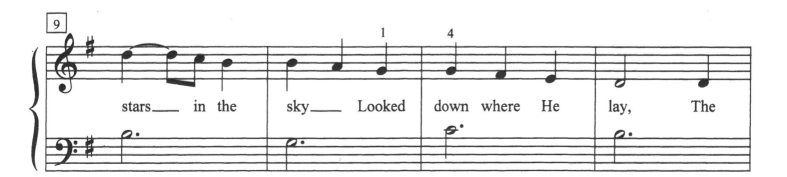

Jingle Bells
Optional Teacher Accompaniment

With energy

Arr. Carolyn Miller

Jingle Bells

Play both hands one octave higher when performing as a duet.

With energy

J. Pierpont
Arr. Carolyn Miller

12603

O Christmas Tree
Optional Teacher Accompaniment

Arr. Carolyn Miller

Moderato

mf

with pedal

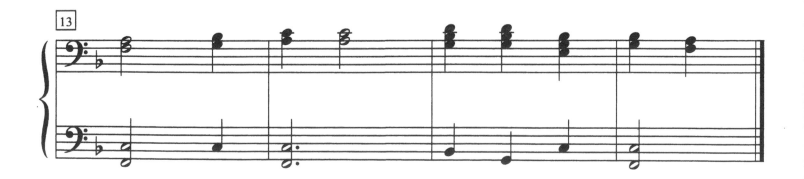

O Christmas Tree

E.G. Anschuetz

German Folk Song
Arr. Carolyn Miller

Play both hands one octave higher when performing as a duet.

Moderato

mf O | Christ-mas Tree! O | Christ-mas Tree!_ Your | leaves are so un-|chang-ing; O

Christ-mas Tree! O | Christ-mas Tree!_ Your | leaves are so un- | chang-ing; Not

on-ly green_ when | sum-mer's here,_ But | al-so when_ 'tis | cold and drear. O

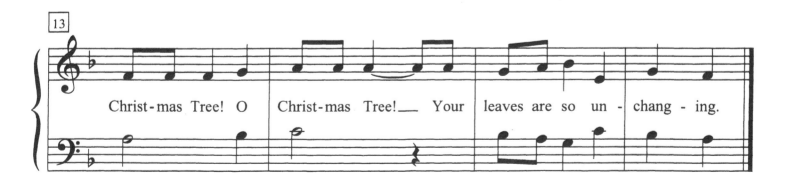

Christ-mas Tree! O | Christ-mas Tree!__ Your | leaves are so un - | chang - ing.

Jolly Old St. Nicholas
Optional Teacher Accompaniment

Arr. Carolyn Miller

With spirit

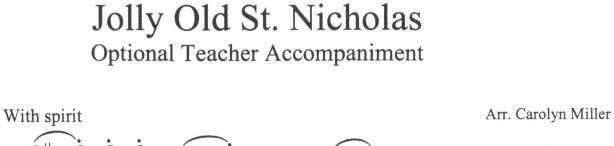

Jolly Old St. Nicholas

Play both hands one octave higher when performing as a duet.

Traditional
Arr. Carolyn Miller

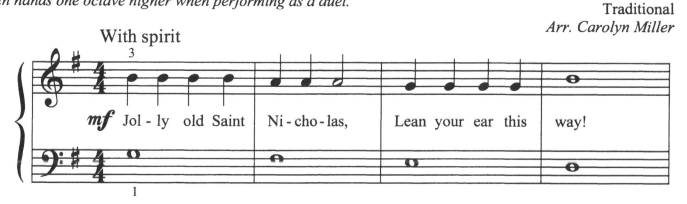

With spirit

mf Jol - ly old Saint | Ni - cho - las, | Lean your ear this | way!

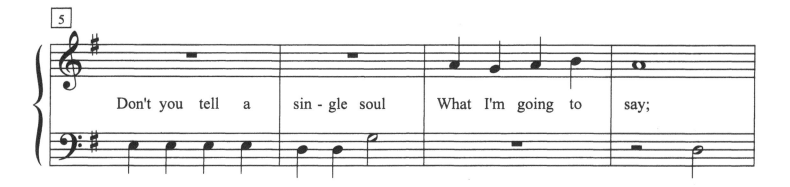

Don't you tell a | sin - gle soul | What I'm going to | say;

Christ - mas Eve is | com - ing soon; | Now you dear old | man,

Whis - per what you'll | bring to me; | Tell me if you | can.

20

Optional Teacher Accompaniment

For variety, try playing the R.H. one octave lower and the L.H as written.
Also try playing the L.H. one octave higher and the R.H. as written.

Deck the Hall
Optional Teacher Accompaniment

Arr. Carolyn Miller

With energy

Deck the Hall

Traditional

Old Welsh
Arr. Carolyn Miller

Play both hands one octave higher when performing as a duet.

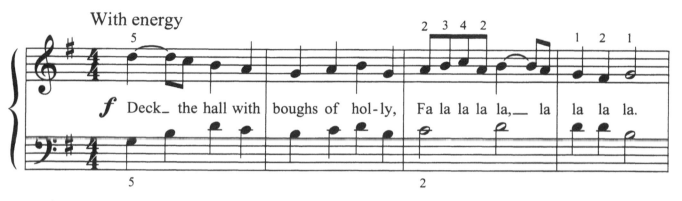

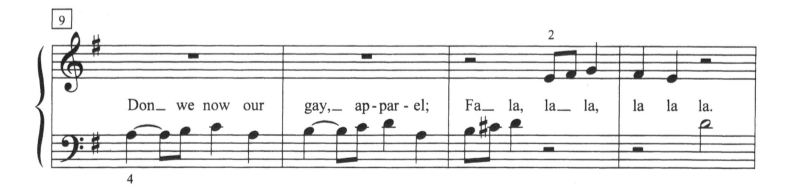

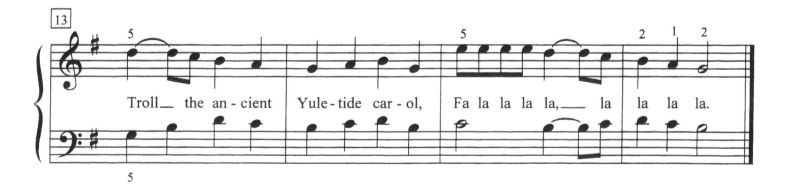